Novels for Students, Volume 45

Project Editor: Sara Constantakis Rights Acquisition and Management: Margaret Chamberlain-Gaston Composition: Evi Abou-El-Seoud

Manufacturing: Rhonda Dover

Imaging: John Watkins

Product Design: Pamela A. E. Galbreath, Jennifer Wahi Digital Content Production: Allie Semperger

© 2014 Gale, Cengage Learning

For product information and technology assistance, contact us at **Gale Customer Support, 1-800-877-4253**.

For permission to use material from this text or product, submit all requests online at **www.cengage.com/permissions**.

Further permissions questions can be emailed to **permissionrequest@cengage.com** While every effort has been made to ensure the reliability of the information presented in this publication, Gale, a part of Cengage Learning, does not guarantee the accuracy of the data contained herein. Gale accepts no payment for listing; and inclusion in the publication of any organization, agency, institution, publication, service, or individual does not imply endorsement of the editors or publisher. Errors brought to the attention of the publisher and verified to the satisfaction of the publisher will be corrected in future editions.

Gale
27500 Drake Rd.
Farmington Hills, MI, 48331-3535

ISBN-13: 978-1-4144-9488-3
ISBN-10: 1-4144-9488-2
ISSN 1094-3552

This title is also available as an e-book.

ISBN-13: 978-1-4144-9274-2
ISBN-10: 1-4144-9274-X

Contact your Gale, a part of Cengage Learning sales representative for ordering information.

Printed in Mexico
1 2 3 4 5 6 7 18 17 16 15 14

Swallowing Stones

Joyce McDonald

1997

Introduction

Joyce McDonald's 1997 novel S*wallowing Stones* is her second foray into the world of young-adult literature. In the work, seventeen-year-old Michael MacKenzie aimlessly shoots a rifle into the air, only to find out the next day that the bullet killed a man who was working on his roof a mile away. The story is told in sections that alternately focus on Michael and Jenna Ward, the fifteen-year-old daughter of the man who was killed. The work thus has two protagonists, both Michael and Jenna, making it somewhat unconventional. Jenna struggles with anxiety attacks after the death of her father, while Michael is consumed by intense feelings of guilt that he compares to the feeling of swallowing a stone. As Michael and Jenna suffer in their own ways, the themes of guilt, chance, and intuition are explored throughout the work, as are the social issues of gun control and teenage mental health. *Swallowing Stones* has been lauded by critics for the emotional depth with which McDonald has portrayed her characters.

Author Biography

McDonald was born on August 4, 1946, in San Francisco, California, but was raised in Chat-ham, New Jersey. Books were important to her from a young age. She has stated that in her childhood, her mother would read to her every night before bed, a tradition that she has kept up on her own ever since. McDonald studied English in college, receiving both her bachelor's and master's degrees in English from the University of Iowa, in 1972 and 1974 respectively.

After university McDonald embarked on a career in the publishing industry. She was a production assistant at Charles Scribner's Sons from 1976 to 1978, a production editor at Springer-Verlag from 1978 to 1980, and a free-lance editor from 1980 to 1984. In 1984 McDonald started her own small publishing press in New Jersey, McDonald Publishing Company/Shoe Tree Press, which she ran from 1984 to 1989. She then went on to work as an editor for Betterway Publications from 1989 to 1990.

In the late 1980s McDonald began shifting her career from publishing and editing to writing and teaching. Her first book, a children's work titled *Mail-Order Kid*, was published in 1988. In 1989 she became an adjunct lecturer at Drew University, in Madison, New Jersey, a position she would hold until 2000. She also worked as an assistant professor of English at East Stroudsburg University, in Pennsylvania, from 1990 to 1996. She went back to school during this time and completed her doctorate in English at Drew University in 1994. While at Drew, McDonald was awarded the Helen LePage and William Hale Chamberlain Prize for her PhD dissertation, "The Incommunicable Past: Willa Cather's Pastoral Modes and the Southern Literary Imagination." The prize acknowledges a dissertation that is "singularly distinguished by creative thought and excellent prose style." During that period she also wrote and published another children's book, *Homebody* (1991), and her first young-adult novel, *Comfort Creek* (1996).

In 1997 McDonald's second young-adult work, *Swallowing Stones*, was published. It was named one of the American Library Association's Top Ten Best Books for Young Adults and one of *Booklist's* 100 Best of the Best 1966–2003. In 2001 she published what is perhaps her best-known work to date, a young-adult novel called *Shades of Simon Gray*. That work was nominated for an Edgar Allan Poe Award. Her young-adult novels *Shadow People and Devil on My Heels* were published in 2000 and 2004.

For eight years beginning in 2002, McDonald taught at Spalding University's brief-residency MFA in Writing Program, in Louisville, Kentucky. She also served for twelve years on the Rutgers University Council on Children's Literature. She lives in Forks Township, Pennsylvania, with her husband, Hubert McDonald, where she continues to write and teach.

Prologue

Swallowing Stones begins with a description of a bullet flying through the air on a hot summer day in the fictional town of Briarwood, New Jersey. A fifteen-year-old girl named Jenna Ward looks up at her father, Charlie Ward, as he is making repairs on the roof of their house. Just as he looks up from his work to wave at Jenna, he suddenly collapses, his body goes entirely limp, and he rolls off of the roof to land at Jenna's feet. It is implied here that the cause of his collapse was his being hit by the previously mentioned bullet.

Meanwhile, on the other side of town a high-school senior named Michael MacKenzie and his best friend, Joe Sadowski, admire the .45-70 Winchester rifle that Michael has just received that day in honor of his seventeenth birthday, which also happens to be the Fourth of July. Because Michael could not wait to fire the gun, he has just shot one single bullet aimlessly into the air. It is implied that that bullet is the same one that hit Charlie Ward. This has taken place during a large pool and barbecue party that Michael's parents have thrown for his birthday, though Joe and Michael snuck off into the woods to fire the gun where no one would see.

The chapter ends with the omniscient narrator

informing the reader that at the end of the day, Michael will reflect on it as the best day of his life because he will not yet know that he has accidentally committed murder.

Chapter 1: Michael

Beginning with the first chapter, the story is told in segments that alternate in focus between Michael and Jenna, the two protagonists of the work. The first chapter follows Michael. The chapter begins early on the day after Michael's party. He has awoken early in anticipation of taking the test to receive his driver's license. As he gets dressed for the day, he reflects on a make-out session he had the previous day during his party in his garage with Amy Ruggerio, a girl from his high school known for being promiscuous, despite the fact that his unsuspecting girlfriend, Darcy Kelly, was also at the party, helping his mother in the kitchen. Michael experiences conflicting feelings about his interaction with Amy. He enjoyed it, but it has made him feel remorseful. Michael eventually puts thoughts of Amy aside to finish getting ready, then heads over to his friend Joe's house. After he wakes up Joe and coaxes him out of bed, the two boys head to the DMV in Joe's Mustang, with Michael driving. In the midst of practice parallel parking the car, the two boys are distracted by a story on the radio about a man in their town being killed by a rogue bullet the previous day. They both immediately realize that the bullet probably came from Michael's gun, though they entertain the possibility that it may have come from elsewhere.

Media Adaptations

- *Swallowing Stones* was recorded as an audio-book, narrated by Ed Sala, and released by Recorded Books in 1998. The running time is 6 hours and 30 minutes.

After discussing the ways that an involuntary manslaughter charge would affect Michael's future, the two decide to make a pact to get rid of the gun and pretend they had never shot it, though Michael feels uneasy about this plan. Nevertheless, he goes home and hides the gun, burying it in his backyard.

Chapter 2: Jenna

The morning after her father's death, Jenna

wakes feeling emotionally numb. She goes about her morning routine indifferently, noticing little reminders of her father all around the house. She goes down to her father's workshop in the basement and reflects upon the events of the previous day in disbelief. She is called back upstairs by her mother, who asks her to help clean the house in preparation for guests.

Soon police chief Dave Zelenski arrives to interview Jenna and her mother about the events of the day before. When Chief Zelenski informs Jenna and her mother that the ballistics team that will try to determine where the bullet came from will not be available until they finish their current case, Jenna erupts in a fit of anger, screaming at Zelenski. She tries to leave the house to go for a walk and calm down but is shocked to find a flurry of reporters and photographers blocking the front of her house.

Chapters 3–5: Michael

The next day, Michael makes breakfast by himself in the kitchen. While eating, he notices a story about the Wards in the local paper and is deeply affected by a picture of Jenna, knowing she is the daughter of the man he killed. His younger brother, Josh, comes downstairs and, to Michael's horror, explains that the entire town has heard about the shooting.

After breakfast, Michael heads to the local pool for his shift as a lifeguard. There he is confronted by his girlfriend, Darcy, who wants to know why he never showed up for their date the previous day. In truth he was so distracted about the shooting that he forgot. While on the lifeguard stand, he reflects on a story he heard about a local girl who died from inhaling a stone in a nearby lake. He thinks that if she had just swallowed the stone, it may have torn apart her insides but she would have survived. To him, keeping what he did a secret is akin to swallowing a stone.

Back at home after work, Michael eats dinner with his family while they discuss the Ward funeral. He leaves to pick up Darcy for a party in the midst of his father's rant about how stupid and senseless the death was. On the way to the party he thinks about how he should break up with Darcy. After overhearing some girls discuss Charlie Ward's murder, Michael makes an attempt to ditch the party but is distracted by Amy Ruggerio on the way out. When the party is broken up by the cops, Michael, his drunk friend Joe, and Darcy all flee.

The next day after finishing his work shift, Michael cannot stand the thought of going home. Instead, he walks around town mindlessly, ending up at Jenna's house. He sits in front of it for several hours. On his way home he comes upon Amy's house by chance. She invites him in. The two accidentally end up spending the night together after falling asleep while playing board games.

Chapters 6–8: Jenna

A few days after her father's death, Jenna

wakes up from a nightmare. She had been dreaming that a local sycamore tree known as the Ghost Tree was attacking her with its limbs. She has had this same dream three nights in a row, which perplexes her because she has never thought of the tree as scary at all.

In the wake of her father's death, Jenna finds comfort in obsessively rearranging and tidying her room and working complex math problems, which distract her and help clear her mind. At her father's funeral, she simply feels numb and does not even cry. Since his death she has only been able to cry in her sleep.

One night a few weeks after the accident Jenna and her mother finally discuss it. They wonder why they have been stricken with this tragedy instead of someone else. Afterward, Jenna goes up to her room and notices that the same boy who has been sitting on the church steps across from her house almost every night since her father's death is there. She does not yet know that that boy is Michael MacKenzie.

The next morning Jenna heads to the pool after being coaxed to go by Andrea. She looks for her boyfriend, Jason Freidman, who has just gotten back from camping with his family. When she finally meets up with him, she notices something very odd—he is making her feel nervous in a way that he never has before. Before leaving she notices one of the lifeguards, who Andrea informs her is Michael MacKenzie, staring at her.

Later that night at dinner, Jenna's mother informs her that the ballistics team has traced the origin of the bullet that killed her father to a four-block area. Desperate to know more Jenna heads to the police station, but she is not able to get any more information there. Not willing to give up, Jenna asks the town gossip, Annie Rico, and quickly learns where the four-block location is.

Later, on a movie date with Jason, Jenna has a panic attack when he slips his arm around her shoulders. In the bathroom at the theater, Amy Ruggerio helps her recover and confides that she has had panic attacks before herself.

Chapters 9–12: Michael

Chapter 9 begins with Michael having a vivid dream that he is a bullet headed toward a man's head. Upon waking, he believes that the dream was caused by his seeing Jenna Ward at the pool earlier that day. He goes into the kitchen and runs into his brother Josh, who informs him that the police are questioning everyone in their neighborhood and who makes a snide joke suggesting that Michael could be the killer. Michael begins to panic internally.

As time goes on, Michael spends more and more time hanging out with Amy at her house. He becomes increasingly attracted to her but tries to resist pursuing anything because he does not want to feel as if he is using her to escape his problems. One night, however, after she asks him why he never tries to kiss her, he finally does. At this point he fully realizes how much he actually likes her and knows that he has to break up with Darcy.

After avoiding Darcy for as long as possible, he is finally confronted by her about why they have not been hanging out and why he has been spending time with Amy. Darcy is furious that their relationship is dissolving and blames Amy for coming between them.

On a stormy night in early August, police officers Doug Boyle and Ralph Healey show up at the MacKenzie house to do some routine questioning concerning the Ward case. They are visiting everyone in a four-block area that encompasses both Michael's and Joe's houses. When asked to produce all of the guns in the house for inspection, Michael explains that he cannot give them his Winchester rifle because he lent it to Joe. When forced to call Joe in front of the police, Michael makes up a story about the gun being stolen out of Joe's car. After the police leave, Michael meets up with Joe, and the boys decide to stick to the story about the gun being stolen.

The next morning, Joe goes to the police station to file a police report about the missing gun. Later that day, when the police come to Joe's house for routine questioning, he tells them the same story.

A few days later Michael goes by Amy's house, only to find her on the front porch, her face blotchy from crying. Later at school he learns that

Darcy and her friends told Amy that Michael had only been hanging out with her as part of a bet to see how much he would be able to manipulate her.

Chapters 13–15: Jenna

One day in mid-August while hanging out with Andrea, Jenna tells her that she has been having a fantasy about shooting her father's killer. At home later that day Jenna receives a letter from Amy Ruggerio. In the letter, Amy explains that she understands what Jenna is going through because she lost both of her parents when she was seven. She says that she wrote the letter so that Jenna would know she is not alone. After reading it, Jenna begins to cry the first tears she has shed since her father died.

That night Jenna has the same dream about vines attacking her, but this time Amy appears in it, leading her to the Ghost Tree. In the morning Jenna's mother tells her that someone has been mysteriously completing chores around their house, such as cleaning the gutters and weeding the garden. This makes both of the women feel uneasy.

Later that day at the mall, Andrea talks Jenna into going to a party. At the party Jenna almost immediately runs into Jason. While the two of them talk outside, Jenna begins to feel anxious. She is thankful when Andrea interrupts them to excitedly inform Jenna that Michael has arrived. Jenna walks right up to his car and tells him that her friend, Andrea, wants to meet him. Jenna's presence seems to make Michael nervous, and he leaves immediately. When Jenna turns around, she notices Amy on the porch watching her.

Chapters 16–18: Michael

At the beginning of chapter 16 it is revealed that Michael is the one who has been tending to the Ward house, cleaning the gutters, taking care of the flower beds, and doing other tasks he believes Charlie Ward would have done if he were alive. One of his other routines has been going by Amy's house to try to talk to her, but so far he has had no luck. On one of his daily runs he spots Amy at the 7-Eleven. He tries to explain that he never meant to hurt her. Though things are still not back to normal between them, Michael feels elated about having reestablished contact.

This feeling quickly dissipates when he arrives home to find a flurry of policemen searching his backyard with metal detectors. To Michael's horror, they find the casing of the bullet that Michael fired in the woods, but are not able to find the gun itself. When questioned about the found casing, Michael claims that he had taken the gun out but had not fired it. He also says that he could not remember whether or not he locked it back up after taking it out. Michael's father says that anyone could have taken it and fired it, and Josh throws out the idea that it was probably Joe. Michael feels guilty for letting suspicion turn toward his friend. He realizes that the police probably never believed the gun was stolen.

The next day the boys meet up and go to the Ghost Tree, in the swamp, so that Michael can fill Joe in in private. Joe is not happy to learn that he is becoming the lead suspect in the case. Because Joe had been drinking, Michael insists on driving them home. On the way, they get into a minor car accident with Amy. Joe flies into a rage, jumping on her car and smashing the windshield, though Michael knows the person he is really angry at is him.

Chapters 19–20: Jenna

After having another dream about the Ghost Tree, as well as Michael, Amy, and this time her father, Jenna reflects on what her father had told her about the tree. Local Native American legend, that of the Lenape, designated it as a place where one could communicate with ancestors. According to her father, it was also a place of healing.

In the morning Jenna and her mother pack up some of Mr. Ward's things to give to charity. On their way out of the house, Annie Rico shows up claiming that she came by to check on them after hearing about new developments in the case. They immediately run inside to call the police department, only to be disappointed by the news that they had not caught the killer but had merely taken a suspect in for questioning. Without telling her mother, Jenna calls Annie Rico to learn that the suspect is Joe Sadowski. Desperate for more information, she goes by Joe's house just in time to see Michael show up at his front door.

Chapters 21–22: Michael

After working a shift at the pool, Michael comes home to the news that Joe has been taken in for questioning. He immediately runs over to Joe's house to hear what happened. He thinks for a moment that he sees Jenna across the street but convinces himself that he is being paranoid, not knowing that it really was her watching him. Joe seems agitated as Michael questions him about what happened. He tells Michael that he stuck to the story but seems less confident that they will get away with everything. In the midst of this, the police arrive to search Joe's house. Michael tells him that if they charge Joe with anything, he will come forward and tell the truth. On the way home he wonders whether or not he would let Joe take the fall for him.

He stops by Amy's house and is surprised to actually find her there, and willing to talk to him. Amy reveals that Joe once told her he had brought her to Michael's party as a gift to Michael, with the expectation that she would have sex with him. She also tells him that the police were at her house that afternoon. Michael comes close to telling Amy the truth about shooting the bullet, but she interrupts him, explaining that she already knows what he is about to tell her. She witnessed him coming out of the woods at his party with Joe and the gun. As they embrace, Michael bursts into tears.

Chapters 23–24: Jenna

At the pool Jenna watches Amy, trying to work up the nerve to speak to her. She senses that Amy knows something about the case but is afraid of what her friends will think if they see her talking to Amy. She finally walks over to where Amy is sitting and thanks her for her letter. The two girls discuss the experience of losing a parent. Jenna is surprised when Amy tells her that the hardest part for her has been living with the guilt that she survived and her parents did not. When Jenna finally works up the nerve to ask Amy about Joe, Amy tells her that she does not believe that Joe is the one who killed her father. Jenna then notices that Michael is watching her and Amy talk, and he looks worried.

Later that night, Jason shows up at Jenna's house and asks to go for a walk. On the walk she finally tells him that she has been having anxiety attacks around him. As they are talking about this, Jason brings up how they had been talking on the phone right before her father's death, a fact that Jenna had completely forgotten. As soon as he says this, the memories of the moments immediately preceding the accident come flooding back to Jenna. She realizes that her mom had been nagging her to get off the phone and call her father in to lunch, but she had not listened. She is suddenly overwhelmed with guilt. If she had just gone to get her father when her mother told her to, he would still be alive.

Back at home Jenna confesses all of this to her mother, who assures her that the death was not her fault. As they discuss the fate of the person whose fault it actually is, Jenna realizes that she knows it was Michael who pulled the trigger.

Chapter 25: The Healing

The final chapter of the book is written in a different style than the rest of the work: it is written in the present tense and follows both Jenna and Michael. The night before Labor Day, Jenna has a dream about the Ghost Tree and her father, except this time she is not being attacked. Her father takes her by the hand, and everything around them disappears except the stars. When she wakes up a few hours before dawn, without thinking about it she instinctively heads to the Ghost Tree.

At the same time Michael is also awake. He knows that he has to confess what he has done and is afraid. He goes outside and digs up the gun. He takes it into his dad's car and drives off.

When Jenna arrives at the Ghost Tree, she senses that her father is there with her. She has come here to say goodbye to him and finally find some peace of mind. She realizes that the dreams she has been having were her mind's way of telling her to come to this place and heal herself.

Meanwhile Michael drives up to Jenna's house. He wants to speak with her personally and tell her what he has done before he turns himself in, as he knows he probably will not have a chance to afterward. When he arrives, he realizes that there is still at least an hour before dawn. Because he cannot think of anywhere else to wait, he heads to the Ghost Tree. When he arrives there he is surprised to find Jenna sleeping at the base of the tree. He decides to wait until she wakes up to talk to her.

Characters

Doug Boyle

Doug Boyle is a police officer also known as the Hangman. He helps Chief Zelenski investigate the Ward case by going door to door to question people.

Jason Friedman

Jason is a boy whom Jenna has been going out with for a few months. She has had a crush on him since the seventh grade. Besides her mother, Jason was the last person Jenna talked to before the accident. Because he left to go camping with his family the day that it happened, he did not find out about it until he returned a few weeks later. Every time Jenna sees Jason after her father's death, his presence inexplicably causes her to have an anxiety attack. Toward the end of the novel, Jenna and Jason realize that her anxiety attacks may have been triggered by the fact that she was subconsciously associating him with her father's death.

Ralph Healey

Ralph Healey is a sergeant on the local police force. Along with Doug Boyle, he is one of the policemen who visits the MacKenzie house for the first time.

Darcy Kelly

Darcy Kelly is Michael's girlfriend. She is known for being one of the most attractive and popular girls at school. After the accident, Michael begins to feel increasingly distant from her and eventually breaks things off. She blames Amy for the demise of their relationship, believing that Michael has feelings for her, and along with her friends begins to bully Amy relentlessly.

Josh MacKenzie

Josh is Michael's younger brother. He is highly interested in the Ward murder case, to the point of fascination. Much to Michael's annoyance, he is eager to keep up with any developments in the case and to aid with the investigation when police visit the MacKenzie residence. He sometimes teases Michael by implying that he is the murderer, not knowing that this is the truth. He is the one who first suggests to the police that Joe may be the culprit.

Karen MacKenzie

Karen MacKenzie, Michael's mother, works at the local florist. Michael worries that she suspects he may be the murderer.

Michael MacKenzie

Along with Jenna Ward, Michael MacKenzie is a protagonist of the story, and he is the one who has fired the shot that kills Charlie Ward. Michael is a well-liked, athletic, and popular soon-to-be high-school senior whose life was fairly normal prior to the accident. He is known for being a big track star at school and a lifeguard at the local pool. He was planning on going to a good college the next year. Though he does not always do the right thing, he is a thoughtful and caring individual. He has always stuck by his best friend Joe, despite the fact that he is much less popular and has some bad habits. He takes care of Joe when Joe drinks too much and helps him stay out of trouble. He is also kind to Amy, whom he has feelings for, even though she is a social outcast.

After he has fired the shot that kills Charlie Ward, Michael's world is turned completely upside down. He is racked with guilt almost every waking moment and has trouble sleeping as well. Even when he can sleep, he has haunting dreams about the accident. He tries to make amends in every way he can think of, keeping vigil outside of the Wards' home and secretly completing chores for them in the dead of night. He constantly feels the urge to admit what he has done but is too afraid of the consequences he will suffer for it. Toward the end of the investigation he has a moment of moral weakness when he considers letting Joe take the fall for him; however, he soon realizes that he could never live with himself if he were to do that. At the end of the novel, he finally decides that he must do the right thing and turn himself in at the police station. But he wants to personally admit the truth to Jenna first.

Tom MacKenzie

Tom MacKenzie is Michael's father. He is outraged by the carelessness of the shooter. Michael worries that, like his mother, his father may also suspect him to be the person who fired the gunshot that killed Charlie Ward.

Pappy

Pappy is Amy's grandfather. He has been her primary caretaker ever since the deaths of both her parents. He is a kind and gentle old man who loves Amy deeply. He sometimes plays cards with Michael and Amy. He is fond of Michael but seemingly oblivious to the fact that Michael has spent the night in his house several times. He protects Amy by keeping Michael away from her when she decides that she does not want to see him anymore.

Annie Rico

Annie Rico works behind the cosmetics counter at the local pharmacy and is notorious for being the town gossip. Early on in the investigation, Jenna goes to her to find out which streets the police have homed in on in the search for suspects. Later,

Jenna asks Annie for information about whom the police have taken into custody as a suspect.

Amy Ruggerio

Amy Ruggerio is a high-school senior who wears a lot of makeup and has a reputation for being promiscuous, even though she is not particularly so. She is a warm and compassionate person but does not have many friends because of her reputation, and thus is somewhat of a loner. Still, she shows up at the pool and parties despite often being by herself.

Like Jenna, Amy has experienced great loss in her life. When she was younger, she was in a car accident that killed both of her parents. Because of this she feels a connection with Jenna and wants to help her in any way that she can. When she sees Jenna having an anxiety attack in the movie theater, she rushes to her aid. She also reaches out to Jenna by writing her a letter describing her own experience of losing her parents.

Amy has had a crush on Michael ever since he and her made out at his birthday party. She enjoys spending time with him, but his ex-girlfriend Darcy attacks her, telling her that Michael only ever paid any attention to her because he thought she would easily have sex with him. After this, Amy distrusts Michael and avoids him, though she eventually comes around to beginning to trust him again when he has a chance to explain that Darcy was lying. Yet around this same time she figures out that Michael is the person who shot Charlie Ward and implies as much to him. She indirectly tells him that he should come clean and that she does not want to see him until he does.

Joe Sadowski

Joe is Michael's longtime best friend. They grew up together. As they have gotten older, Michael has become significantly more popular than Joe, whose behavior and appearance are frowned upon by some of his classmates. He often wears a bandanna around his head and a dangling skull earring. He drives a Mustang, from which he blares loud rock and metal music. He has difficulty expressing his emotions in a healthy way and is a heavy drinker despite the fact that he is several years too young to drink legally.

Joe was the only person who was with Michael when Michael fired the bullet that killed Charlie Ward. He and Michael were also together when they learned that Charlie Ward had been killed by a stray bullet. Joe convinces Michael that they should keep the fact that Michael shot the gun a secret, thereby voluntarily incriminating himself as an accessory to the crime. Joe adamantly believes that if the police cannot locate the murder weapon, they cannot charge Michael with murder. Yet when questioned about the whereabouts of his rifle by the police, Michael reports that he let Joe borrow it, casting direct suspicion on him. As the investigation progresses, Joe is taken down to the police station for questioning and becomes the primary suspect in the case. Even still, he sticks to the story the two boys have fabricated about the gun being stolen and does not rat out his friend.

Andrea Sloan

Andrea has been Jenna's best friend since they were little. They grew up as neighbors. She is described as being attractive and fairly popular at school. She is a good friend to Jenna and tries to lift Jenna's spirits after the death of her father by coaxing her to go out to the pool and to parties. She has a crush on Michael MacKenzie and often persuades Jenna to accompany her to events on the grounds that he might be there.

Charlie Ward

Charlie Ward, the father of Jenna Ward, is killed by a stray bullet at the beginning of the novel. He was enthusiastic about his tools and worked in upper management at AT&T.

Jenna Ward

Jenna Ward is the other protagonist of the story, besides Michael. She is the fifteen-year-old daughter of Charlie Ward, the man whose murder is the catalyst for the entire story. She was present at the time of her father's death and actually witnessed the bullet hitting his head and his falling off of the roof. She had always been closer with her father than her mother, as she and her mother sometimes do not see eye to eye. She is a good student and well liked at school. Like Michael, she led a fairly normal life prior to the death of her father.

After the accident, she has a difficult time accepting what has happened. It is almost as if her brain cannot process the fact that her father has died. She cannot remember anything that happened directly before his death. She also cannot cry about the incident and has trouble feeling much of anything at all, aside from sporadic bouts of anger. She also has dreams about the Ghost Tree and Michael which she believes are related to her father's death. She is obsessed with the idea of finding her father's killer and does some detective work of her own when she cannot get the information she wants from the police. She wants revenge on her father's murderer.

Jenna obsessively organizes and rearranges her bedroom and works complex math problems as a way of calming herself down when she begins to feel overwhelmed. A few days after the accident, she begins to suffer from anxiety, particularly around her boyfriend, Jason, who was the last person she spoke to before her father's death. It is not until Jason reminds her that he was talking to her on the phone right before the accident happened that her memories begin to return and her anxiety begins to dissipate.

Thanks to her own detective work and the intuitive connection she feels with Michael, toward the end of the story she realizes that he is the one who killed her father before he has a chance to tell her. Once she knows this, she can truly accept that her father is dead and begins to feel a sense of peace. She no longer wants revenge.

Meredith Ward

Meredith Ward is Jenna's mother and Charlie Ward's widow. She is an account executive at a large New York advertising agency. She and Jenna have a somewhat strained relationship due in part to her type A, hyper-organized personality. However, over the course of the novel they bond over the loss of their family member.

Dave Zelenski

Dave Zelenski is the local police chief. He keeps Jenna and her mother apprised of any developments in Charlie Ward's murder investigation. He is middle-aged and rather large.

Themes

Guilt

Guilt, particularly the guilt associated with the loss of a loved one, is a major theme in *Swallowing Stones*. It affects the majority of the main characters. When Jenna and her mother have their first heart-to-heart talk after Charlie Ward's death, Meredith Ward expresses the deep remorse she has over having been unable to prevent the accident. As she explains, she is overwhelmed with the feeling that if she had done something differently, her husband would still be alive.

Topics for Further Study

- Read the young-adult novel *Lovely, Dark and Deep* (2012), by Amy

McNamara. Like several of the characters in *Swallowing Stones*, the protagonist of this novel, Wren Wells, is dealing with the trauma of losing a loved one. Think about how Jenna and Wren are similar or different in the ways that they deal with trauma and loss. Then write an essay comparing and contrasting the two characters.

- When Jenna is feeling upset and overwhelmed, she retreats to her bedroom to work complex math problems. For Jenna, math has a therapeutic effect. This is only one of many surprising applications for mathematics. In fact, there are many connections between math and the world of the arts. For example, some artists use mathematic formulas to generate patterns or determine the size scale of a work. Using the Internet, research an artist of any kind (visual, musical, dance, etc.) who has implemented mathematics in his or her work. Using a camera and video-editing software, create a short film explaining to your fellow classmates how the artist you have chosen uses math. Be sure to insert visual aids such as pictures or graphs into your video.

- The death that serves as the focal point of *Swallowing Stones* was caused by an accidental gunshot wound. Every culture has a different way of approaching the subject of gun control, and every country has formed different laws to regulate guns. Research the history of gun-control legislation in the United States as well as in another country of your choosing. Create a PowerPoint presentation with information demonstrating what you have leaned. Be sure to include slides explaining how gun laws in the two countries are similar and different.

- One of the themes of *Swallowing Stones* is chance. Sometimes there is no discernible reason for an event like Charlie Ward's death, it is just a matter of coincidence. Choose one detail of the story, large or small, to change. Then write your own alternate ending based on how you imagine the story would be different as a result of the detail you chose to change.

Amy, who was in the car with both of her parents with they died from a crash, confides in her letter to Jenna that for her, the hardest thing about losing her parents was the overwhelming feelings of guilt. This was initially surprising to Jenna, but Amy explained she somehow felt guilty that she was the one who survived. Amy suffered from a phenomenon called survivor's guilt, which occurs when a person feels that one has done something wrong or unfair by surviving when others did not.

Because Jenna initially suffers from the post-traumatic stress of having watched her father be hit in the head with a bullet and fall to his death, she initially does not feel guilty or even very sad. She mostly feels numb but goes through bouts of feeling shocked, angry, and anxious. Toward the end of the novel, when she begins to uncover the cause of her anxiety, feelings of guilt come forward to replace those feelings. She suddenly feels as if she was the cause of her father's death because she did not go out to beckon him inside as soon as her mother told her to. Just like her mother, she begins to experience the guilt of having been unable to save her father.

Michael, on the other hand, experiences a totally different type of guilt—the guilt of taking another man's life. While Jenna and her mother only feel as if they were the cause of his death,

Michael actually was. Moreover, he also feels guilt over constantly lying to everyone around him about what he has done. These feelings of guilt eat away at him, until eventually he cannot stand it any longer and knows that he has no choice but to come clean.

Chance

The concept of chance is another theme that is explored in the work. Charlie Ward's death is characterized as a freak accident because the circumstances were so unusual, and because there was no possible way that it could have been predicted. Oftentimes human beings like to feel as if there has to be some order to life, as if there is a reason behind everything that happens. Sometimes when bad things happen to good people, they begin to search for a potential reason. They believe they are being punished in some way. Yet Charlie Ward did nothing to deserve to die, his family did nothing to deserve to lose him, and Michael did not intently do anything to deserve the punishment of becoming a murderer. Charlie Ward's accidental death was merely a matter of chance. Michael's circumstances cause him to fully realize that his fate is entirely out of his control and that, to a certain degree, control is always an illusion.

Intuition

Amy and Jenna, the two characters in the novel who have lost parents, are also the characters in the novel who are highly intuitive. They are able to sense other people's feelings, particularly feelings of pain, nonverbally. Their intuition plays a major role in the novel, as it draws them each toward one another, and toward Michael. Even before Jenna knows Michael by name, she feels connected to him. For example, when she sees him sitting on the church steps across from her house, she senses that they share a similar type of pain. He also turns up in her dreams quite often, indicating a subconscious connection. And toward the end of the novel Jenna realizes without being told that Michael is the killer. At this point she and Michael are drawn to the Ghost Tree at the exact same time. Amy also feels drawn toward Michael, and he toward her. Their unlikely friendship prevails despite the fact that they are both teased for it. Additionally, Amy senses Michael's secret and the pain he is carrying far before she lets on. Finally, Amy and Jenna connect on a deep intuitive level as soon as Amy reaches out and writes her letter to Jenna. They are the only two characters in the book who fully understand the type of pain each other is feeling. Furthermore, Jenna senses that Amy knows something about her father's death that she is not saying.

Style

Symbolism

The most evident example of symbolism in *Swallowing Stones* is the Ghost Tree. The Ghost Tree is surrounded by local folklore and legend and is said to have healing properties. While it does serve as a symbol for healing throughout the novel, it also encompasses all of the pain that goes along with the healing process. Throughout the novel Jenna has a recurring dream that the tree's branches are coiling around her, restraining her body. The pent-up emotions associated with her father's death that she is not able to express while conscious are manifest in these dreams. Michael also feels drawn to the tree throughout the book. He ends up going there several times without ever realizing that he is heading there until he has nearly arrived. It is almost as if the tree is seeking out both Michael and Jenna in their states of emotional trauma. In the final chapter of the book, the two instinctively go there at the same time to confront their demons. Both are finally ready to begin the healing process.

The other major symbol in the book is the figurative stone that Michael has swallowed. After the accident, he remembers an incident a few years before when a young girl suffocated to death while playing a game in the lake with a friend. The two girls were diving down to the bottom of the lake and picking up stones with their teeth, when the young girl tragically inhaled one. Michael remembers thinking that if she had just swallowed it, it would have damaged her internally but she would have most likely survived. To him, the secret of his killing Charlie Ward is like a stone he has to swallow and carry around with him as it tears him up on the inside. However, at the end of the book he realizes that actually he has been carrying the stone around in his throat the entire time, and the work of swallowing it will be to admit to everyone what he has done.

Multiple Protagonists

Swallowing Stones has two protagonists, Michael and Jenna, who are both equally important to the story. A protagonist is the main character of a story and is typically the character that readers most closely identify with. While it is not unheard of for a novel to have more than one protagonist, in literature it is more common for a novel to have a single protagonist. Because the portrayals of Michael and Jenna are equally vivid and both emotionally salient, the reader can empathize with both and will not necessarily favor one over the other, or identify with one more than the other. Though Michael may initially seem like an antagonist because he committed an accidental murder, it is obvious from the beginning that he had no intention to kill anyone and is absolutely horrified that he did. From the way McDonald chronicles his internal struggle, it is clear that readers are meant to sympathize with him, not despise him for what he has done.

There are pros and cons to creating a story with multiple protagonists. While having more than one main character can aid in the development of a complex plot, some readers do not appreciate works that have multiple protagonists because they tend to make the meaning of a story less straightforward and to pull the reader's sympathies in two, sometimes opposing directions. However, this is a matter of personal taste.

Gun Culture in the United States

Swallowing Stones is centered around an accidental death by gunshot. Unfortunately, in the United States death by gunshot, accidental or otherwise, is far from unheard of. As Michael A. Bellesîles notes in his 1996 article "The Origins of Gun Culture in the United States, 1760–1865,"

> An astoundingly high level of personal violence separates the United States from every other industrial nation…. The weapon of choice in 69.6 percent of those murders [in the United States in 1993] was a gun, and thousands more are killed by firearms every year in accidents and suicides.

In fact, the United States has the highest rate of gun ownership in the entire world and also has some of the most lenient gun-control laws. In some places in the world it would be unthinkable to give a seventeen-year-old a firearm for his birthday, but in suburban New Jersey, where the novel is set, it does not seem unusual at all. Michael is eager to show off his new rifle to his friend Joe.

Compare & Contrast

- **1990s:** Between 1990 and 1999, there are twenty-three mass shootings in the United States. One of the most widely covered shootings, the 1999 Columbine High School massacre, prompts a national debate about gun-control laws.
  Today: In the wake of seven mass shootings in 2012 alone, including the Aurora theater shooting and the Sandy Hook Elementary School shooting, the gun-control debate is just as widespread today as it was in the 1990s, if not more so.

- **1990s:** According to the US Centers for Disease Control and Prevention (CDC), from 1990 to 2003 the rates of suicide among young people ages ten to twenty-four steadily decrease.
  Today: A 2007 CDC report reveals that in 2004, 4,599 children and young adults committed suicide, an 8 percent increase from 2003 and the largest increase in suicides among young people in fifteen years.

- **1990s:** In 1999, Georgia becomes the first state to pass anti-bullying legislation to help protect students such as Amy who suffer emotional distress at the hands of their peers.
  Today: As of 2012, forty-eight states have passed anti-bullying

laws.

Mental Health Issues among Teenagers

Swallowing Stones depicts a group of teenagers who are dealing with different types of mental health issues and emotional distress. Jenna experiences intense grief and anxiety attacks after the death of her father. Michael struggles with the overwhelming guilt of having accidentally killed a man. Joe deals with the stress in his life by turning to alcohol. Amy, who has experienced the deaths of both of her parents, describes struggling with survivor's guilt. She is also mercilessly bullied by her classmates, who falsely accuse her of being promiscuous. Although these instances are of course fictional, they are representative of a very real and long-standing problem in the United States: the high rate of emotional distress among teenagers. The teen years are a highly formative time not only physically but also mentally. The majority of mental health issues diagnosed in adults have their roots in adolescence, and over half of all diagnosed cases of mental disorders begin by age fourteen. According to the National Adolescent Health Information Center, as of 1995 (two years prior to the publication of *Swallowing Stones*), a survey indicated that among young people ages twelve to seventeen in the United States, 16 percent of males and 19 percent of females "met most of the diagnostic criteria in the **DSM-III** for one of three psychiatric diagnoses—major depression, post-traumatic stress disorder, or substance abuse/dependence disorder." Additionally, as of 1999, nearly 25 percent of young people ages seven to sixteen had one or more emotional or behavioral problems.

Depression has been the most widely reported disorder among teens in the United States and is almost twice as common among females. The cause of depression in teens varies from case to case and can sometimes be difficult to determine, but the effects are often tangible and evident. Depression has a negative impact not only on the individual suffering from it but also on that individual's friends and family. It is particularly dangerous in that it can lead to other concerns, such as substance abuse, self-harm, and suicide. Anxiety disorders are also prevalent among teens and often occur in conjunction with depression. Conduct disorders, learning disabilities and attention deficit/hyperactivity disorder (ADHD), and eating disorders are also significant problems among teens.

Critical Overview

Swallowing Stones, McDonald's second young-adult novel, received a flurry of critical attention upon its publication in 1997, though it has not been heavily addressed by scholars since. By and large critics lauded McDonald's ability to make the emotional states of her characters resonate with readers. For example, in a review of the work a contributor to *Publishers Weekly* claims that the portrayal of the characters' emotions is true to life and one of the strongest parts of the novel.

The contributor comments, "While the novel's sequence of events is rather farfetched, the characters' reactions are real. Readers will quickly become absorbed." Other critics likewise claimed that McDonald's vivid characterization is a feat unto itself. Joel Shoemaker, who reviewed the work in *School Library Journal*, observes, "This mesmerizing story largely derives its power from the respect McDonald demonstrates for these teens and their emotions."

In another contemporary review, a *Kirkus Reviews* contributor also notes the characters' emotional journey as one of the most significant aspects of the book. Although the contributor describes the ending as somewhat "awkward," overall the reviewer calls the work a "deliberately paced but deeply felt drama." This reviewer was not the only one to take issue with the ending, which varies in style and tone from the rest of the work. *Booklist* contributor Frances Bradburn writes in her review, "McDonald masterfully moves both teens to an inevitable, if somewhat nebulous, final confrontation." Indeed, Bradburn cites the ending of the work as its only weak spot.

Nevertheless, reviews were generally positive. *Book Report* contributor Brooke Selby Dillon cites "believable and empathetic characters; fascinating minor characters, who defy stereotypes;" and "poetic, haunting, yet easily accessible language" as some of the main draws of the work. Dillon concludes, "McDonald has crafted a gem."

What Do I Read Next?

- *Izzy, Willy-Nilly*, published in 1986, is a young-adult novel by Cynthia Voigt. Like Swallowing Stones it addresses how one accident can change a person's life instantly and permanently. After fifteen-year-old Izzy loses her leg in a car accident, her entire world changes.

- *Devil on My Heels* is McDonald's 2004 young-adult novel. Protagonist fifteen-year-old Dove Alderman has a relatively easy and happy life in 1959 Benevolence, Florida. Yet when fires begin breaking out around town and rumors of Ku Klux Klan activity spread, Dove's sense of security and safety in her town begins to waver.

- *The 1997 book Guns, Violence, and Teens*, by Vic Cox, is an overview of the place of guns in American society with particular attention to how guns affect young people. The author covers both sides of the gun-control debate equally.

- Sherman Alexie's 2007 young-adult novel *The Absolutely True Diary of a Part-Time Indian* is about Arnold, a Native American teenager who leaves life on the reservation to attend an all-white high school. Though at first Arnold finds life at his new school difficult, he eventually finds ways to fit in. Outside of school, Arnold struggles through many hardships over the course of the novel.

- *Speak* is a 1999 young-adult novel by Laurie Halse Anderson about a high-school freshman who is ostracized by her peers after calling the police at a party. What she does not tell anyone is that she called the police because she was raped.

- In McDonald's 1996 young-adult novel *Comfort Creek*, eleven-year-old Quinn and her family endure a string of bad luck. Her mother has left the family to play in a band, and her father has lost his job.

Sources

Bellesîles, Michael A., "The Origins of Gun Culture in the United States, 1760–1865," in *Journal of American History*, Vol. 83, No. 2, September 1996, pp. 425–55.

"Bio," Joyce McDonald website, http://www.joycemcdonald.net/bio.html (accessed April 15, 2013).

Bradburn, Frances, Review of *Swallowing Stones*, in Booklist, Vol. 94, No. 4, October 15, 1997, pp. 397–98.

Cox, Ruth, "Unspoken Words—Words Left Unspoken," in *Emergency Librarian,* Vol. 25, No. 5, May–June 1998, pp. 46–48.

Dillon, Brooke Selby, Review of *Swallowing Stones*, in *Book Report*, Vol. 16, No. 3, November–December 1997, pp. 37–38.

Follman, Mark, Gavin Aronsen, and Deanna Pan, "A Guide to Mass Shootings in America," in *Mother Jones*, February 27, 2013, http://www.motherjones.com/politics/2012/07/mass-shootings-map?page=2 (accessed May 1, 2013).

Heise, Jennifer, "Helen LePage and William Hale Chamberlain Prize," Drew University website, https://uknow.drew.edu/confluence/display/DrewHis (accessed May 1, 2013).

"Joyce McDonald," Random House website,

http://www.randomhouse.com/author/19835/joycem sort=best_13wk_3month (accessed April 15, 2013).

"Joyce McDonald (1946–) Biography," Brief Biographies website, http://biography.jrank.org/pages/1877/McDonald-Joyce-1946.html (accessed April 15, 2013).

Khazan, Olga, "Here's How U.S. Gun Violence Compares with the Rest of the World," in *Washington Post*, December 14, 2012, http://www.washingtonpost.com/logs/worldviews/w shooting-how-do-u-s-gun-homicides-compare-with-the-rest-of-the-world/ (accessed May 1, 2013).

Knopf, David, M. Jane Park, and Tina Paul Mulye, "The Mental Health of Adolescents: A National Profile, 2008," National Adolescent Health Information Center, 2008, http://nahic.ucsf.edu/downloads/MentalHealthBrief.j (accessed May 1, 2013).

Lange, Sydney, "Birthday Bios: Joyce McDonald," Children's Literature Network website, http://www.childrensliteraturenetwork.org/birthbios/4jmcdnld.html (accessed April 15, 2013).

McDonald, Joyce, *Swallowing Stones*, Ember, 2012.

Review of *Swallowing Stones*, in **Kirkus Reviews**, July 1, 1997, https://www.kirkusreviews.com/book-reviews/joycemcdonald/swallowing-stones/ (accessed May 1, 2013).

Review of *Swallowing Stones*, in *Publishers Weekly*, September 1, 1997, http://www.publishersweekly.com/978-0-385-

32309-3 (accessed May 1, 2013).

Ruff, Morgan, "*Shades of Simon Gray*," Prezi, February 12, 2013, http://prezi.com/syiedmoulzuz/shades-of-simon-gray/ (accessed April 15, 2013).

Sacco, Dena T., Katharine Silbaugh, Felipe Corredor, June Casey, and Davis Doherty, "An Overview of State Anti-bullying Legislation and Other Related Laws," Harvard Law School website, February 23, 2012, http://cyber.law.harvard.edu/sites/cyber.law.harvard. (accessed May 1, 2013).

Shoemaker, Joel, Review of *Swallowing Stones*, in *School Library Journal*, Vol. 43, No. 9, September 1997, p. 219.

Webber, Carlie, "Joyce McDonald: Interview," Teenreads.com, July 2004, http://www.teenreads.com.asp1-14.dfw1-2.websitetestlink.com/authors/au-mcdonald-joyce.asp (accessed April 15, 2013).

Further Reading

Feinman, Jay M., *Law 101: Everything You Need to Know about American Law*, 3rd ed., Oxford University Press, 2010.

> *Law* 101 is a comprehensive and engaging introduction that will familiarize readers with the American legal system. This work will help readers understand the charges Michael would be up against if he were to be tried for involuntary manslaughter.

Krementz, Jill, *How It Feels When a Parent Dies*, Knopf, 1981.

> In Krementz's book, eighteen children and teens share their experience of losing a parent. This book is designed to comfort youths who have experienced the loss of a parent and also to illuminate the experience for others.

Salmore, Barbara G., and Stephen A. Salmore, *New Jersey Politics and Government:* The Suburbs Come of Age, 4th ed., Rivergate Books, 2013.

> Barbara and Stephen Salmore's book educates readers about the culture of New Jersey, where *Swallowing Stones* is set, and the politics that

made it the way it is today.

Souter, Gerry, *American Shooter: A Personal History of Gun Culture in the United States*, Potomac Books, 2012.

> In this work Souter provides a history of gun culture in the United States through the lens of his own personal experience. Souter was raised with guns and is himself a gun-sport enthusiast, but he is highly critical of some current aspects of gun control.

Suggested Search Terms

Joyce McDonald

Joyce McDonald AND Swallowing Stones Joyce McDonald AND YA fiction Swallowing Stones AND YA fiction YA fiction AND gun violence

Swallowing Stones AND gun control Swallowing Stones AND teens AND guns loss of a parent AND survivor's guilt involuntary manslaughter AND gun-control laws involuntary manslaughter AND guilt